SECRET CHORDS

A Poetry Anthology of the Best of the Folklore Prize

www.folklorepublishing.co.uk

SECRET CHORDS

A Poetry Anthology of the Best of the Folklore Prize

An anthology compiled by
MARTIN CONNOLLY

FOLKLORE PUBLISHING

Selection, introductions and notes copyright © 2021 Martin Connolly.

Copyright of the poems rests with the authors and Folklore Publishing Ltd until the end of 2021 and with the authors alone thereafter.
ISBN: 9798701734911

First published 2021 by
FOLKLORE PUBLISHING LTD
ELAINE COURT, 123 HAVERSTOCK HILL
LONDON NW3 4RT

www.folklorepublishing.co.uk

This collection copyright Martin Connolly © 2021

Martin Connolly has asserted his right under the Copyright, Designs and Patents Act 1988 to be identified as the owner of this work.

Cover design: Martin Connolly

Cover image: Saul and David by Albert Adams (1956) reproduced with permission from the Estate of Albert Adams

*for Jehane, Seán, Piers, Poh Sim, and Merlinn, for their
help, love, and support, and for poets everywhere*

CONTENTS

Foreword by Martin Connolly

I ask poets everywhere to forgive me for first saying that without the guidance and collective wisdom of Piers, Seán and Jehane, none of this would be possible. I am deeply grateful for all their support, for going on this journey with me, and trying to inspire conversations with poets and writers everywhere. To the writers and poets – thank you for entrusting us with your work, and I hope you don't mind if I am now handing it over to the reader, as it is theirs now, and I hope it brings comfort as a companion and travels well and far.

This competition began as a way to bring some solace and comfort to people in lockdown and isolation, to help promote wellbeing and spark creativity in people who needed an outlet. I hope to some degree it has been successful, and thank you to all of the poets, students and stars of the National Health and Poetry Service, commonly known as the NHS, who contributed. We received such a high volume of entries that we could have filled several anthologies, and the degree of talent made it extremely difficult for our judges to narrow down the winners and those selected for inclusion within these pages.

To everyone whose work is listed here I offer my congratulations and thanks, especially to those who won, but also to everyone who entered, and entrusted us with their work. In embarking on this project, we have found an incredible community of writers. We acknowledge that leap of faith is not easy to do, and while we could not print every single poem, there are memorable and beautiful poems not within this book which we know will find a home in due course. No one should be dismayed or give up hope for entering other competitions, especially the young writers who have so much talent. To those who entered but are not printed here, my advice – while I am in no position to judge the quality of anyone else's work – is to keep going because the talent is staggering, and the effort will be rewarding.

Seamus Heaney said that writers live at the intersection of the public and the private, and it's not easy to put your work on display – our notes on the contributors towards the end of the book will give you an insight into the diversity and range of writers who have put themselves forward in this project. Keep in mind that each of you, dear readers, brings the same poem to a new life – no poem is read the same way twice. Yet it is only when art – like that of Albert Adams, to whom we dedicate this anthology – is encountered by an audience that it is fully born, wholly alive, and the same holds true for poetry. The same, in fact, holds true for music. These are all secret chords, and together maybe there is some hidden meaning behind the music, behind everything that we went through together in the pandemic.

I hope the competition spurred some people into more creative writing that helped them cope with the lockdowns and trials we faced in the past year and encouraged others to pick up books of poetry they had not read for some time, and rediscover old favourites and meet new ones. If we have achieved that, we have achieved a great deal that we can be proud of.

Poetry itself is not a competition – this prize began as a way to spark a conversation, inspire and give a new lease of life to people during a dark period. I hope more books like this will emerge, more emerging voices will be heard, and poets will support and promote each other. This book is a small companion, a little insight into the talent that is out there in every walk of life, so take it, own it, and hopefully, to paraphrase Seamus Heaney again, you might find something in it that catches your heart off guard and blows it open.

Martin Connolly *is a business consultant in procurement and social value, writer, volunteer, and founder of Folklore Publishing. He was also elected as a Governor for his local NHS Trust, The Royal Free NHS Foundation Trust, representing constituents in Camden, Barnet, Enfield, and Hertfordshire. He is originally from Ireland and lives in Hampstead, London.*

An Introduction from Seán Street

Those of us who have been fortunate enough to have had the opportunity of reading all the entries submitted for this inaugural Folklore Poetry Prize found ourselves on a journey into inner worlds that expressed so many moods and emotions, so many forms and shapes on the page, and so many vivid explorations of language, that (I know I speak for my fellow judges here) while it has been an enriching, heart-warming experience, it has not been an easy one.

After all, how do you make choices between excellence? How am I – who am I? – to declare a hierarchy given such quality and various stories? I console myself with the thought that in the end this has not been a competition but a conversation, and importantly, a conversation that probably could only have taken place at this extraordinary moment in global and personal history.

The cumulative effect of reading these poems is a deep reassurance that in the midst of the maelstrom, there is a rich and caring humanity. Justice, empathy and a sense of history are themes in so much of the writing. Personally, I have particularly loved the poems that made me as a reader engage through an intensity of image and language, poems that took me to mental and emotional places in which, while sometimes I might have felt that I was being taken on a voyage I didn't fully understand, I was always held by the compression of thought, and the blend of the personal and the universal in the guiding idea behind the writing.

The best poets, like the best doctors, are attentive to the symptoms of circumstances and situations. They do more than hear – they listen. They do more than look – they see.

So, in congratulating not only the winners and the others included in this book, I also pay tribute to everyone who took the trouble and care (in every sense of the word), to write and offer their work to us.

And if I may, I'd like to offer in return a poem as part of the conversation, towards the advocacy of staying tuned to the wonder in the everyday, and the humanity that we celebrate in the work of the authors within these pages.

Seán Street is writer, poet, and broadcaster. His most recent poetry collection is Camera Obscura (Rockingham Press). A new sequence, The Sound Recordist, will be published by Maytree Press in 2021. Prose includes works on Gerard Manley Hopkins and the Dymock Poets, as well as books on radio history, and a number of studies of sound poetics, the latest of which, The Sound of a Room: Memory and the Auditory Presence of Place, is published by Routledge. He is emeritus professor at Bournemouth University.
www.seanstreet.com

Dutch School
Cardplayers in a Sunlit Room Pieter de Hooch (1658)

So often there is a door opening, a fold
of light like this, sky or another place sometimes
beyond us but awaiting attention, the hold
day has when it is shone aslant spare chequered rooms.
I saw nothing to remark on until you said
look, trained me to see the timeless in normality,
these buried domestic unknowns opening wide
the human, its everyday informality.
Yes, just like that, expanding ordinary space,
changing it as an approaching figure crosses
a yard to temper time with her indistinct face,
but a living face on a threshold nonetheless.
A moment: our days exchanged as she enters, while
energy alters like a reawakened smile.

SEÁN STREET

An Introduction from Jehane Markham

During lockdown something changed within my work. It got better. Poetry was holding my hand. All the normal structures of life had folded. No friends in the house, no going to the pub, no grand kids to kiss and cuddle. My workshops had stopped, and no public readings were possible. So, when Martin asked me if I would co-judge a poetry competition that he had set up with Piers Plowright and Sean Street I said yes, without a moments' hesitation. I just wanted to be close to poetry and this was a way to support what I thought was a really authentic grassroots idea of encouraging people to express themselves and their thoughts, fears, dreams, in this frightening time of isolation and deadly virus. As Seán says, I like to think of it as a conversation rather than a competition and I would like to thank everyone who had the courage and energy to send in poems. It makes a stunning collection. I am grateful for my fellow judges for their collaboration and for Martin for carrying through the idea with such care and discernment.

Jehane Markham is a poet, lyricist and dramatist. She works across all media from radio, theatre, television and performance poetry. She has worked with musicians and created several musical dramas with contemporary composers. She had her own Trio for ten years performing The London Series and Vladivostok to Moscow. She has published four pamphlet collections of poetry and has run poetry workshops in London and Norfolk. She was poet in residence with The Camden New Journal for three years.
www.jehanemarkham.co.uk

Tenement Building, New York

There was a humming in my head all day long;
it was Aunt Ida working the treadle of the sewing machine

and a sour smell
from the blue tongue of gaslight

that hissed through the glass cup.
I was afraid of the raised iron

with its dragon eyes –
"Tush, tush, tush,"

and ma would pass by with her big skirt swishing
but she didn't pick me up.

There was a loaf on the table, like a golden plait
and gherkins, fat as thumbs in a jar.

The kettle whistled when it steamed and boys
whistled up and down the ironclad stairs

delivering cloth and collecting garments
for the up-town stores.

Once father burnt himself lifting the tin pan:
boiling water splashed up

red as fresh strawberries
on his white skin.

Then ma wrapped the arm in a wet cloth
and he sat down and wept like a man.

JEHANE MARKHAM

An Introduction from Piers Plowright

Twelve days after the first UK lockdown in March of 2020, I wrote a poem called The Room that expressed how I felt. And then I met Martin Connolly, neighbour and now friend. He was volunteering for people like me and my wife Poh Sim and dropped in a free anthology of poetry. Something to feed body and soul. And opening us all up to the power of poetry in times of trouble. So, when he suggested running a new poetry prize, I was honoured to be one of the three judges, along with Hampstead-based poet Jehane Markham, and poet, scholar, playwright, and radio guru now living in Liverpool, Seán Street. This book contains the winners and a selection of some of the best entries. Long live Poetry.

Piers Plowright is a radio producer, writer, and artist. During his time as a BBC radio drama and feature maker from 1968 to 1997 he won the Prix Italia for radio documentaries three times as well as three Gold and two Silver Sony Awards and a Sony Special Award for Continual Dedication and Commitment to the Radio Industry. Since then, he has been made a Fellow of the Royal Society of Literature, an honourary doctor at Bournemouth University and a 'Radio Luminary' at the prestigious Chicago Third Coast Radio Festival. He is married to Poh Sim, formerly lecturer in Oriental Drama at Royal Holloway College and a big influence on his work. They live in Hampstead, London.

The Room

Let's look at it again
Now there's no escape:
Those books you half-remember
Photos of the kids
The chair that's caving in
And the tiny miracles
Of light and shape
You failed to notice –
Business forbids
The attentive eye and heart–red tape
Now you've all the time you need
So let's sit still. And then begin.

PIERS PLOWRIGHT

When My Mother Says Jamaica
(After When they say Connemara by Geraldine Clarkson)

I see scrubland, a hill of gravestones
near a blighted crop that leads towards
three wooden steps of a tumbling shack.
Underneath are boxes, there to hold it up,

split at the sides, soaked through by humid storms,
the dwelling like a boat at times – three rooms adrift;
eight children reaching for a father
who longs for rum enough to call it his *best friend*.

When my mother washes clothes by hand,
she becomes a girl again, kneeling at a stream,
beating rags on sheen-smooth rocks,
sleeves rolled up her muscled forearms.

They turn to fat when she migrates to England.
For now, the stream rolls over them,
her mother standing close,
holding up a length of cane pulled from the fields,

to bring down on a cringing back
if suds aren't plentiful enough. The stream calls out,
Make that girl work like a slave.
Grandmother hears so many voices bubble up.

They're in the soil telling her to beat her girls
as she was beaten by her father for being much too dark.
He is *almost* white and *married down* –
a woman brown as a dead leaf.

That's how he describes my great-grandmother
who's not allowed to call him Earl but
Mister Hargreaves – headmaster with a length of cane.
He brings it down on cringing backs to teach a *ragged mob;*

slave masters offered discipline, each one a hero to this man
who stays out of the sun, pale skin shaded by a hat
that hides the shame of kinky hair.
His daughters call him *Sir;*

place coins upon his eyes to keep the corpse
from following his wife about the room. She cries
until he's safely in a grave; then laughs.
That's what my mother says when she talks of home.

JENNY MITCHELL
Winner of the Folklore Prize

The Window

A small bird perches on the kitchen chair,
timid, full of hope, looking back
at the way it flew in – the window someone closed.

I remember my mother alone, holding on,
watching her fingers flick like chaffinch wings,
dreaming of her garden.

I wander past the dog sprawled on the red sofa,
photos of my children, shelves of poetry
and carry on upstairs, return to the highest room,

just as I left it – Rembrandt-dark, scent of lavender,
wooden floor silent, a candle, ceramic horse for company,
my notebook abandoned open at the page

of good intentions. The day I would write
until sunlight bursting through the attic window
was all that mattered.

KERRY DARBISHIRE
2nd place winner of the Folklore Prize

Haggerston Waste
In memory of Rashan Charles

Even before he died, the boy was
a chalk-line shape, his thin limbs holding

onto the ground, his fingers spread out
across the tiles, the elbow at a right angle

reaching towards the fridge door.
The man's left leg is also on the floor,

also a right angle, but the rest of him
leans on Rashan, his right arm

tucked under the boy's neck – the film shows
a struggle on the floor, Rashan is spun

towards the fridge, knocking some bottles
onto their sides, and his thin legs

dangle, his blue jeans cut from the sky.

HARTLEY LLOYD PACK
3RD place winner of the Folklore Prize

Fledging the Rainbow
(for Ian)

Your celandine room: how it lights
my way home, the sleet-drizzled lane

and all the greys of winter breathing round,
lead oxide, snow-wolf's hair.

Nearer to, I'll hear you. These branches:
your strings. These wrens: minims

and over the frets your deft hands fly –
tailpiece to headstock, gold plectrum

as if you're Clapton, Iommi,
hints of Santana, Thin Lizzy

all the rogue heroes, a sunbow of sound,
blues to flamingo, love's prism

as if you're born with aerilons,
as if your wings out-span this time

its lockdowns relieved,
its dank outplayed. As if

my heart's a runway. As if
a thousand tints of sky are freed.

LYNNE WYCHERLEY
Recipient of the Highly Commendable Award

Wash Day

That young woman, whispering to herself,
is my mother, hair still black, Monday,
all day smelling of wet washing. She feeds
the rubber rollers of the new electric mangle.

Limp things drop into the cream enamel bucket
that stood for twenty years inside
our spidery outhouse. The kitchen walls,
later painted glossy lilac, are still

that turquoise green. In one corner
stands the warship-coloured oven, toecaps
of cast-iron. The sun comes out, yellowing
the afternoon. Our cat yawns on the back lawn.

In a line dance from the rusting post
are bed sheets, wide clothes, little clothes, alive
in wind. All gardens run toward the long
wire fence against unbuilt-on fields.

She begins to sing to the steamy air
three coins in the fountain ... humming through
some unremembered words, pausing
to begin again. Nothing else matters.

A bunch of pink carnations wilts
in the cut glass vase, a wedding present.
It's chipped now, somewhere in my loft,
beside her illustrated book of British birds.

GREG SMITH
Recipient of the Highly Commendable Award

Sister is Still and Light

Sister bruised against him.
Her cheeks were milk roses,
soft hair longer than he remembered.

Cremation day was still, cold.
The doorway was a slit,
voices of the congregation

cool and crystal as holy water
the place a bright blur
of blooms gone rogue;

yellow orchids, titanic lilies
in hot pink, heaving
with God's odour.

After it was done,
Brother tried to catch her,
calling over the valleys,

her voice a blood-thin song,
the crematorium disappearing
in the rear-view mirror.

Brother drove in the dark,
hair wild, clawed out.
He drove, counting road kill,

waited with her by the lake,
breathing in her vase of
ash and slivers of bone.

NATALIE CRICK
Recipient of the Highly Commendable Award

Nostalgia

I remember the two lime barrels
left in the box of Black Magic
we had given our mother for Christmas

with the exact same nausea now
as then, the early 70s, when,
with the Quality Street long gone

I was desperate enough to risk one.
Naïve enough to believe that since last year
Rowntree's might have improved things

and a sweet lake of caramel would break
to spread across my tongue, releasing
a crunchy roasted hazelnut, but no.

The same vile lime aberration, year in
year out. And now I come to think of it
perhaps this nostalgia I'm feeling

is for my mum, who was young then
with over half a century
of life ahead. And though she knew nothing

of this, my memory has her celebrate it,
by standing at the window, staring
into the distance, where none of her children

could reach her, should she fathom a way
to go there. She peels the cellophane strip
from a pack of Embassy Regal,

saying *I swear you kids will be the absolute
death of me.* And she strikes a match
that lights up her face, sudden, and lovely.

VANESSA LAMPERT
Recipient of the Highly Commendable Award

We Take Our Son to University

Inside the car
we feel the rhythm of the road; the keening of the wheels
plays upon the skin.

Outside,
the morning is everything October can be - a liquid
brightness
so clear and sharp it cuts; its beauty pains the eyes.

The sky is cloudless;
above the lines of the fields the red kite wheels, slices
through the air, an effortless moving away from us.

The road signs
mark our progress, like the counting down to the moment
of launch,
when you go out into the Universe.

Ten miles left,
conversation stalls as the power station's cooling towers
come into view,
scab on the horizon of an otherwise perfect landscape.

We fall to
unfamiliar silence as the slip road drags us to the end point
and like the red kite, you lift off and soar away.

BETH BROOKE
Recipient of the Highly Commendable Award

Hold on February

when I was five I trimmed my hair with nail scissors
　　　　on tiptoes
I observed my errors in the mirror.
you whisked me to your hairdressers on kings lane to
obscure the damage.

here we sit again,
　　　　amongst hot blows,
to conceal yours,
a joyful bell mocking us as people enter.

Silver scissors delicately snip what has not fallen,
your own roots abandoning you
through no fault of their own.
your identity wilting,
tufts swept away by a tarnished brush,
still harbouring the pained strands of those before you.

I want to swallow all the unspoken sorrow of each hack,
　　　　swelling *my* abdomen,
　　　　snagging *my* arteries,
　　　　my erythematous skin bruised
　　　　with premature grief

I ask for a blunt cut above the shoulders
to relieve the prolific weight,
but the severed detachments prickle my neck,
　　　　the type that cling to you despite showering

I pay for the both of us,
lashes crusted with precipitated salt,
cheeks streaked with black.

29

you assess your reflection and smile,
and I've never loved you more,
I wish I needed tiptoes to see mine,

>   *take me back,*
>   *take me back.*

ZARA AL-NOAH

Watching crows in the field on a frozen morning

Through February's stillness
of cold and crispness of clear,
hawking cries of strong, black
warriors fight each other out throatily
to win their share of clean mid-morning chill.
Tar-gleaming muscular chests
and hoarse wild calls strike
coarsely off each other like sea salt.

Their proud, warrior feathers
(each one sewn to another, living as a whole),
sliced. By the expert swish of a samurai's sword,
as morning sunlight sweeps from within,
as it must: powerful, instantaneous.
Harsh and welcome, it cuts
blindingly across feathered armour.
And resounds back and out;
jaggedly breathtaking
as the rare and dangerous
crystal cuts of ice on the flat roof below.

One sits lofty and alone
on a thin, bare branch
of wintered birch. Calling
upwards to no one.
From branch to claw to heaving chest to tipped beak to sky.
As if he knew he were made to be solitary.

Crying to be alone
and crying not to be.

BECKY CIESIELSKI

The Nights of My Life Come and Go

Do you remember the March night
of the snowfall, the bright moon, everything swan-white?
I crept out of bed to find you washing plates, lost in
thought, while you waved for me to stand beside you,
the scene at the window, and watch the garden fill up with
snow.
I can still see you motion to the window, your hesitant
smile.

The nights of my life
Come and go.

The snow was on each blade, our pines, the hawthorn,
and from the scrapbook of my childhood is torn
that picture of us, your arm gently wrapped around me.
I later absorbed the way you stood, the accent in your voice
and the way you walked, as if I ever had any other choice.
Like a movie still inside me, our last picture show, by heart
a scene I know.

The nights of my life
Come and go.

And something unsaid was troubling you.
Maybe tomorrow would bring something new
but that moment, we watched in silence the growing snow
bury our trees - all growth stopped - our garden grass
and God, I hoped the moment would not pass.
Did you hear me say I loved you, unutterably low?

The nights of my life
         Come and go.

RANDALL STEPHENS

After Grenfell

It was the strangest thing,
finding an empty nest
on the busy street
as I made my way
to, of all places,
the Muslim Cultural Heritage Centre
to donate.
Wondering if I should have worn something else,
or if it was ok to just be myself.
The nest was empty,
but I tried to think happy thoughts
of how they'd grown,
all survived,
cuddled through chilly April,
watched the darling buds of May,
and flown off, peaceful doves.
But, as this was Notting Hill,
more likely pigeons.
But no. I cannot smile.
We cannot all be ready when we fall.
The vision of your handkerchief at the window,
breaks my heart
into unequal, torturous, horrified parts.
I walk, humbly, into your arms.
Take this bag, please, and love me.
I know it is not enough.

CIORSDAN GLASS

Dizzy

Bedtime used to be easy
she would fade before nightfall
her head heavy against my shoulder
as I carried her down
now she pleads
to stay up just a little longer
she has so much to do
the world, still being new
to an eight-year-old

some nights I relent
her Pied Piper pleas
an irresistible song
I ask her to choose one thing
just one thing to do before bedtime
she tries, she really does
but she cannot
at the end of the day
everything is magic

so, we pull the stars down from the sky
fling them at the wall
and see what sticks
last night we played dominoes
the night before that we listened to our favourite songs
tonight, she just wanted to talk
she cleaned her teeth on her pogo stick
before bouncing into bed
I tucked her in, held her hand

she asked me to tell her something new
something that she didn't know
she closed her eyes, ready
in whispers I told her that the world is hurtling through
space
spinning quickly all the while

in the hush, she asked me
why we don't get dizzy
I squeezed her hand goodnight and told her
that sometimes, we do

STEVE DENEHAN

Shelling Beans

In the hazy sunshine, the old tin saucepan in front of us,
We sit on the doorstep and shell beans.
They thud softly, pauses in our laughter.
Sheep murmur in the distance,
A background noise to our constant chatter,
As we plan our time together, heads
Bowed to the job in hand.
The case of the beans is velvet soft,
And I ask to keep one to make a bed for the faeries.
Light glints on your glasses as you
Turn to smile, knowing it will be discarded
By tomorrow for a different game, but say,
Shall we make a pillow and blanket, too?

HELEN OPENSHAW

Dreaming

My mother's pinafore was blue and streaked with fat
Her sleeves rolled up she sprinkled flour upon the rolling
pin
The kitchen table swayed and then the cat
Flew in and hid inside a basket full of gleaming pods of
peas and then jumped out
And watched my mother fill the tin
With pastry and some frothing egg, then dot it all about
with ham
And red tomato
Then in oven gas mark 4
Oh how I would adore
To be there now and shell those peas and pick a bunch of
mint
Which grew under the washing line where handkerchiefs
and pants
And socks hung in the sun
If I had a dream of being young
Then I would run and run and fling my arms around that
pinafore,
My mother and the years before.

PETRA MARKHAM

Switching on my electric blanket at 2am

I climb the stairs with the light foot of a burglar
Close the door behind me without moving the air
Switch on the small lamp, the cream lamp, the floor lamp
Switch on Dreamland that warms the empty space beside
me
Whatever happened?
Your pillow looks puzzled
I sigh without thinking
I occasionally swap it over
But it doesn't smell of you
Whatever happened
To the marshmallow of love
When we couldn't touch enough, couldn't laugh enough,
couldn't live enough
So softly and softly words became fewer
The space between them crept up on us like a thief
And our days became the drip of a tap
Into an empty sink
We're the same people aren't we?
So whatever happened?
I thought the wine in our cellar
Would be sweet and soft
Saved for dessert
Drunk slowly with the dust of memories undisturbed on
the bottle
But our glass is undrunk
And the sweet grapes of yesterday
No longer for drinking
But for cooking

RICHARD PILKINGTON

Fifty-Three

You are tired.
And your back hasn't seen a good day since you left the
civil service,
But there's no changing you now.
You are an old boy by trade, none of this funny business.
Cash in hand, sometimes kept off the books.
Set in brass and sold off like copper.
You grumble under your breath,
You, exhale.

There are fumes from a plastic bag burning on the
underside of your car.
Bacon grease has set into the passenger seat, and an old
lion is hanging by a withered blue rope to the bumper.
Rotten apples are hiding beneath your bonnet, the juices
sting your tongue.
Your throat barks.
The scent of diesel and propane are thick in the summer's
heat.

You are lost in the eclipse.
One that follows three-hundred years of endless sun.
It did not burn your skin; you doubt it burned mine.
One of your shoulders hangs lower than the other, thirty
years of leaning on a bar.
Your fingers instinctively curl inwards.
Arena air clogs your lungs, but you could not breathe
without it.

You are a bull dog's pup.
You are the product of a handbag that has been passed
down through generations.

The boys that once ran with you on cobbled stones now
take the tube.
And there is a gentleman on the platform who sounds
familiar.
Like a headmaster you used to know, or a matron who
taught you how to tie your shoelaces.

And just like that, it is 5.30 in the morning again, and you
still have fourteen years left until retirement.

You are tired.
You, exhale.

AMY GILLIES

The bench which waits

Like the towers it faces,
it has a place,
Rooted in the uneven grass,
Slabs, slippery from the dew
Waiting for conversation,
Observing city lights, lined
Like candles on a birthday cake,
But as there is no celebration
It watches and waits.

Waiting for watchers,
It wants to offer weary legs
And hungry eyes a place,
To unpack the picnic of the view,
But its etched letters do not call
To these hurried people,
Armed with purpose, masks and sticks,
Their fragile defence against the invisible,
The air loaded with fear.

It fears the loneliness
Echoing with the owl's howl
It feels the sadness
Weeping behind railings,
As the garden bursts with unseen buds of beauty.
But the isolated bench feels the warmth of Sunlight,
The only one refusing to hide behind a shield
So they play patterns, angular games,
And wait for friends to come again.

CORIANDER STUTTARD

Next Second, You Were Gone

I heard about an old broken phone box
Where people would go to have imaginary conversations
At first, I found it foolish
And then I joined the queue.

When my turn came, I dialled your old number.
There was no ringtone, but I told you everything
and I waited in silence
as if you might respond.

I thought I heard you breathe.
Then I remembered they told me my life should go on.
One second, you were here.

RANDALL STEPHENS

Pantoum for Changing Weather

The earth is tilting, longer nights will shake the walls
leaves like ripped out pages are falling through the rain
and we don't know who we are anymore,
where we will be when the nights are short again.

Leaves like ripped out pages are falling through the rain.
There never was a time when we could say for sure
where we will be when the nights are short again
who will be in power next year, who will fall.

There never was a time when we could say for sure,
when the powerful, consumed by greed, aren't sane,
who will be in power next year, who will fall.
There is just this: days and the weather change.

When the powerful, consumed by greed, aren't sane
and we don't know who we are anymore
there is just this: days and the weather change
the earth is tilting, longer nights will shake the walls.

DOMINIC FISHER

The Necklace

My mother
      holds
the necklace in her hand,
      a gift
from the grandson
      who loves her.
She has forgotten
      (again)
that it is hers.

She sits, twists the
      rope
around her fingers,
      explores
each bead, the knots
      between.

This object of her
      veneration
is like a rosary of her
      life,
each bright decade a
      set of
memories she
      can no
longer thread into
      biography,
but which held in the
      hand
is marvelled over,
      made new
with every touch.

BETH BROOKE

His Second Book

Hard-won maturity. Exuberance
  Married to intuition. Mastery
Of form without the sacrifice of sense
  Plus wit to make the wheels turn faster. He

Has "got his act together" -- but would never
  Be crass enough to put it thus. His goal
Is to be useful not just snidely clever.
  Triumphantly this book fulfils that role!

Who, then, deserves our thanks besides the bard?
  His mother or his muse? Both do, no doubt,
    But also the far-seeing one who nursed

The plant from seed to crop and took the hard
  -- Or so it seemed – decision to bring out
    Before his wondrous second book – his first!

ROBERT ILSON

Teenage Girl

her body is a sphinx
several parts girl,
several parts dog, dragon, bird
her neck is a flower stem
she is the enigma

he has dreamed of girls before
too scared to riddle their girlhood
too scared of their breastwell, cheekflush

his girl wears a crown, red and gold,
chats razors to her brothers
loves the sun

too scared to tear pages from her books
he wrinkles hair ribbons in his pockets
in the lonely hours

her front door is red
her Mam looks like a whore
her plush carpet is plusher than his own
her bedroom is like a brothel
he wants to sing a song for the dark

too scared of the petals that will shed
he leaves no marks, he does it quick
and too scared never thinks of it again

too scared, never speaks of this
he did it to her and it was -

NATALIE CRICK

Curvature

Sometimes I stand in the
      sea, stare at the horizon,
            and imagine you are
      across the water, looking
back. If it weren't for the
      Earth's curvature, maybe
            our eyes would meet as we
      scanned the skyline, maybe
we could be together.

              What is it like where you are?

The remains of a crab wash
      up on the shore, pecked open
            by gulls; its back blood-eagled,
      pincers splayed out in surrender,
the scent of the deepest
      ocean trench echoing inside
            its exoskeleton. Do things die
      on your beach too? Would this
creature have survived there?
      Barnacles dry up by the rock
            pools, sinking into themselves
      until the tide comes, brings
them back for a time, owing
      everything to the moon's revival.
            Periwinkles scatter like broken
      bitumen, each one turning to
face the horizon with me.

Sometimes, I stand in the
        sea, not sure if I should
                start walking towards you,
        cross this barrier to find
you smiling on the other side.
        As my feet slip into the
                sand, an epiphany strikes:
        if it weren't for the Earth,
I could see you.

BRIONY COLLINS

The Fall of Stalingrad, 2020

there's Al,
ranting,
smashing up small porcelain figurines on the pontoon,
stamping them into bits into the wooden slats,
shouting about Stalingrad
and the Russian Front,
again.

I wanted to KILL her
he says
about a passing cyclist who stared too long at the scene,
take clubs to skulls
like they did in LA
during the riots.

So much life and death
and violence and geography
for a morning on the canal
late for work
in Nottingham.

DAVE BEVAN

What's in a Name?

I am often asked,
Why does your father have an English name?
Isn't he from China?
Isn't he Chinese?
If only you knew the ignorance stemming from your
thoughts, branching out of your mouth and dripping down
into your words. If only you knew the pain that strikes
from those.
China, a country I've never seen. Never been.
It is the birthing country, a motherland.
But you are Chinese? Yes and no.
I am a daughter of Hong Kong. The harbour of incense.
Island children found to the south. Where we speak in
Cantonese and drink milk tea.
Shaped by being an old colony, traded under duress. By
your country.
By my country. The one I own a piece of. The one I was
born in.
My father has an English name because it made life easier.
For foreign tongues not to twist and choke. For foreign
tongues to not learn their place. To accommodate.

S.M.L. YAU

His Name Escapes Me Right Now but It Might Come Back to Me Later

They gave him everything
water torture
sleep deprivation
they starved him
removed his fingernails
the fingers themselves
his ears
they peeled parts of his forearms and thighs
dripped acid onto his feet
cut words across his chest and stomach

his motorcade had driven
too close to enemy lines
he had been captured
a bounty, a piñata
bulging
with military secrets

held for months
presumed dead
forgotten by most
until his body
what was left of his body
was returned

it is believed
that he gave them nothing
that he endured it all
everything they had
and gave them nothing
maybe nothing was all he had to give

maybe it was that simple
either way his family
their knees worn smooth from prayer
got him back

at his funeral there were flags
and a twenty-one-gun salute
that frightened his son
his family were given a medal
in lieu of his bravery
it was shiny

STEVE DENEHAN

Eve

Eve is ready. From her earlobes hang solar systems
- opulent globes, ascending in size, reaching for her
shoulders. Her lips, slicked sticky, shine with brand-
new gloss. She has gems in her nose,
on her great slinking sleeves, and on her throat
there sits a hulking diamond, cut brilliant so
she breathes out spectrums. Her body, melodic,
jingles. The dress licks, smooth lining loving her
like freshly slept-in sheets, cool and soft,
and her eyelashes curl up always. From the quick
apostrophe of her mouth, her voice
spills: collected rainwater, unfiltered gifts. She is big,
has to duck through doorways, yet light on her feet.
Eve walks every step as if about to spring into a
dance – shoulders back, calves tensed, eyes forward.
Effortless. Her front teeth rest on her bottom lip.
She stands at her front door, flung wide open, toes
pressed to the threshold. She scents the night wind,
leonine. The cold sneaks into spaces left by the
setting sun. Manicured hands laced behind her back;
she rocks on the balls of her feet. Three insistent
curls bounce from her neat chignon, teased by the
day's sigh as it slumps away. Eve puts on her patent
heels and stands by the mirror; not checking it, she
lights a cigarette. She takes one draw and holds it as long
as she can
then   releases. The
murky tendrils drape around her like snakes on
runway models. Eve licks her teeth and stubs out
the cigarette in one, decisive pat. Her coat puts itself
on, expensive weight working like a man's gent-
eel arms. She swishes through the door, pauses;

tonight is going to be a good night. A mist of stars
flirts with the streetlamp glow. She walks, and her
stiletto-on-ice clicking lulls the world into
suspended animation.

REBECCA BAIRD

The Lych Way

Endings are never final. We have them all the time.
The end of a song, of a love, of a day.
When people pass, we walk the lych way.
It's different everywhere.
In the gorse-choked moor it's marked by stones
Like the bones of fallen giants.
The city is built of nothing but carcass,
Steel, not stone, but who's counting?
It's corpse roads are harder to find.
But if you look long enough, you'll see
Where the wagons once rolled over granite
As hard and cold as their cargo.
In the country, some fields lie fallow forever.
The lych way marches through,
Frost in their silent wake.
The dead don't talk much, anymore.
Their graves have become our pavement
And footfall drowns them out.
Once we feared them.
We wrapped our graveyards in tangled topiary
To keep them from spilling out.
Now the cities themselves are labyrinths
Of streetlamps and grey disaffection.
We fear the living now.

MAX HALLAM

Summer, 2020

I was pretending to read
that time
those times
we laid in the sun
there was nothing to do but read
and read
roll over and read
you kept me entertained
I followed the raspberry seeds
on your chest
and the line on your hip -
the game it played
between the cool and warm
of your skin.
I did not read at all.

NICOLE CHARLESTON

just five more minutes

criss-crossed and tied together
like laces, in the shoe of our slumber
early, on an alarm-free Friday morning

the dancing hand of a crisp breeze
reaches in from the window ajar
and teases the warmth from under the duvet

gentle hums and rustles of the city
are muted by grey velvet cushions
far too big for a double bed

morning birds make shadow puppets
and the sunlight curls around us
like a cat wanting to be stoked

day isn't in a rush to begin
and a grin spreads across my face like butter
thoughts of breakfast plant their feet

I taste the sweet reminiscence from the night before
and lose my fingers in his gorgeous curls
that smell like jasmine, orange, love

his breath twirls around my neck
and I peck his cheek
wishing for just five more minutes
with him asleep
because I'm not finished
this beautiful dream

SARAH JANE O'HARE

2020

A song with friends, a touch – so much we miss
How fast our world's become disoriented
2020 wasn't meant to be like this

As night draws in, we zoom and reminisce
On things we took for granted, now lamented
A song with friends, a touch – so much we miss

A time of crisis – news we can't dismiss
Despair and fear – so many so tormented
2020 wasn't meant to be like this

Perhaps we'll better see what's been amiss
Now that each day has to be invented
2020 wasn't meant to be like this

One day we'll rise with hope from the abyss
Into a fairer world we've reinvented
2020 wasn't meant to be like this

The world could be much wiser after this
Connection's what we need to be contented
A song with friends, a touch – so much we miss
2020 wasn't meant to be like this

DANUTA ORLOWSKA

Little Fish

Let me hold your hand
and squeeze just a little, just enough.
Let me place my hands around the base of your neck
to warm you, wick away the rain, the outdoors.
Let me draw you a bath, with salts and oils
tinctures and potions to soothe you.
Let me warm you, with water, with coffee, with skin.
Let me hold you, my sweet little fish, softly softly in even
softer light.
Let me reduce the noise, turn down the garish brightness
of your day out there.
Let me serve you, as you serve them.
I'll bring you food, imperfect and ugly but made with my
whole heart.
Let me be your cradle, your church, your sanctuary.
While the world screams outside the windows
we'll watch the condensation cloud it from our view.
In our nest, our nook, our burrow beyond sirens and
strangers.
Pull the curtains, dear heart, and wrap your limbs around
mine.
We'll lounge entangled like dozing lions
watching the candles grow short.
Watching our shadows dance tall.

BETH FINNEY

Making Biscuits with Cassandra

I have not walked down the aisle
Focused on the single horizon
Of a love about to blossom into
A long-awaited sense of forever

But I have woken suddenly from exhaustion
Into perfect wakefulness
When the young ex-prisoner came and sat beside me
Eager In the rehab centre
To show me the poems
He had read to no one
ever.

I have not seen my children
Come back from their first day at school
to tell me about the friends they made
The snacks they lost, the teacher they're scared of
The new library ticket with their own name on

But I have stood on the brow of a hill alone
With a sense of an impossible arrival
As the fog poured through the Golden Gate bridge
In the morning in San Francisco.
I'd come to study 'existentialism in film, novel and drama'.
In a place I had only known in a movie, in Berkeley
California.

I have not found you waiting for me after a long day
Knowing that I have been chosen to belong here
While forever lasts in this passing world.

But I have taught Cassandra to make zoo biscuits
With specially coloured icing on top
That we made ourselves
And I've witnessed her telling me
With all the authority
Of her 6-year-old solemnity

"Sarah, I could go on making these biscuits
For the rest of my life"

SARAH DE NORDWALL

Pike
(Esox Lucius)

Jealousy
        is a pike
resting in sleepy shallows
amongst twisted reeds, gnarled roots
ever vigilant in gloomy shadows,
elongated green speckled body
camouflaged, fins tickling the surface.
It will curl and spring without warning,
catch you in its mouth,
there is no way back.
Swallow you whole.
You need to fish carefully -
Sit with patience and time;
and on a grey day,
catch him on your hook;
He will fight hard, twisting
and retching, spinning the line.
Bring him in close, scoop up your net,
stare face to face at this fragile creature
then choose to let him go.

CAROL SHEPPARD

sit with me here

sit with me here
on the grass
watch the trees wave
in the wind
they know
you're here
to say
goodbye
don't you know
you fill me with joy?

CHRISTINA LEWIS

A Villanelle: A Lament for Summer Gone

The summer's gone, the clocks go back tonight.
Tomorrow we will all adjust the time.
I hate this morning gloom, I need the light.

Now fallen leaves and rain put joy to flight.
And all our dreams we'll have to redesign.
The Summer's gone, the clocks go back tonight.

With lock-down blues we feel there's no delight
We're stuck in mud, the will to act declines
I hate this morning dark, I need the light.

Escapist stratagems now all seem trite.
The play we planned is just a simple mime.
The Summer's gone, the clocks go back tonight.

We cannot see our friends as is our right.
The rules constrict, enjoyment is a crime.
I hate this morning gloom. I need the light.

Give me I beg some small thing to excite.
A takeaway meal and a glass of wine
The Summer's gone, the clocks go back tonight.
I hate this morning gloom, I need the light.

JIM MULLIGAN

How Could She?

That summer unspooled
itself into September.
I made damson gin and jam
from my father's trees, they had not reacted well
to uprooting and a new home.

For nine years they had hesitated,
until a sharp cold spring
brought the surprise of late May flowers,
which wrote I.O.U.s
for this autumn fruit.

We drank the gin at Christmas,
toasted his memory.
I promised myself
not to mind the loss,
that without ceremony

had taken up a permanent corner
in the room whose door I kept ajar
to creep into
when I needed to be with him,

as I do now,
when language is as unknowable
as the spite that chopped
down his trees.
It's not like they were yours

ANNA BEDDOW

Jesus H. Cormorant

there's Jesus up on the cross.
and there's the Shags up on the orange buoys;
classic crucifix death pose
prostrate, drying their wings
in the trent valley winds,
resurrected anew
ready to scavenge and
fish these holy waters
for just what they're worth.

life imitates art
imitates life
eternal.
when the symbols shatter
let us cast them all
to the river.

DAVE BEVAN

Glass

When I was laid up with a broken leg,
you visited me once. I saw you through
the bay window, but when you rang the bell
I didn't make it.

Soon I was swinging around on crutches,
and they chucked you out of school for smashing
some arsehole over the head with a chain,
and you moved away.

Then I was standing on my own two feet,
making a mess of things most of the time,
while the cripple in me spent twenty years
hobbling to the door.

J.D. MURRAY

Travelling to Find Her

I hoped to find her,
All I had was an old hairband,
Stretched from the years
I'd held it on my wrist,
I told the pilot to take me,
Wherever the winds drove us,
Where the clouds parted,
The air was strong up here,
I wondered what it was like down there,
I hoped her hair was ok

She always worried about her hair

LIBBY CHANDLER

Shining
Covid Ward

I imagine you there, I
don't know where, but I
see your white hair pasted to
your tired head,
still shining.

I wonder if your hands with
yours and Grandma's gold bands still
mix the air like conducting wands,
beauty and elegance
still shining.

Mum the teacher, JP
Am Dram, moral preacher. Intensely
private, yet sociable creature.
Determination
still shining.

You can see my eyes, no
gown, goggles, gag can hide my
trying smile, face shocked wide to
find you so
depleted.

Permission to come, the doctor said.
Dad, unwell stays home, prepared to
phone-whisper a devotion shared for
three score years and one
today.

Then one last time for his 'Princess' a
gentle touch provides caress as
piano keys transcend distress... and
I see your eyes
are shining.

SAM SMITH

Transfer

I don't know what it feels like
to lose half of who made you
to a virus that passes like poison through some
and like water through others.

But I know what it is to witness
the slow shedding of responsibility
to a partner
to a child and
to themselves.

Like pieces of armour dropped in disarray
on life's forest floor.

I watch mutely as his daughter trails after him,
moss mapping her footsteps.
Affixing to her limbs each piece of unoccupied armour
and trying on braver and braver faces
until she no longer recognizes the one in the mirror.

I don't know what this feels like,
and neither do you.

Yet you hover in the half light
as a new leader is born.
Offering your hand when the role feels too heavy,
candle wax dripping onto your skin
as you walk with her into the night.

You can't imagine, but you don't try to.
Your words are plain but constant
I'm here, I'm not going anywhere,
I love you.

When the terrible transformation is complete,
your pace never falters.
Dawn blushes through the canopy overhead
and her steps are
a little lighter
for your
presence.

AOIFE O'CONNOR

Smoke and Minnows

for St George's School, founded in Ramsgate in 1841
now rebuilt in a more rural setting

He wanders lonely through the fug
the slenderised boy with saltpetre cheeks
garnering rods of offcut glass from the Works.
For bait there's fish glue from the boil-up man
who squats to dip my knotted parcel string.
On the gasworks pier, we anglers angle
our transparent sticks and imagine fish
gliding the bombed site translucently,
find a third lung with which to breathe
piscine adhesive and vitric miasma.

And then the toiling of the bell, the counting-in
at our blessedly incensed school;
Closed Windows, Open Minds – our motto.
There we learn: the physics of fumes and vacuums,
how the Goths caught the Romans' coughs,
and The Feudal System – which Mister Rowan said
allowed oppressed serfs fresh air
divided into strips and centuries later
to take up the mantle of Britannia and catch
the breath of the world on Drake's heels.

(More...)

(Continued...)

74

Worst times, outside windows are hosed
twice in a day to move the smudges
to new positions, just the way troops
are deployed in war, our teacher believes.

The school's noose tightens in calm weather.
Some days the seaside breeze spells reprieve
in gusts of seafront candyfloss and sun oil.
One day the hangman will hang the school
on a hook and lifts it like a Dover sole.
We'll look out on fields of daisies.

PHILIP BURTON

Mrs. Fairfax

I should have been flattered
she thought I was the mistress
despite my -----shire accent,
but as I said to her, I never presumed.
I'm no snob, I didn't object,
though I was surprised at first.
Such an age gap. Of course I never knew
he had a wife already, don't you think
I'd have said something if I had?
If, as he told her, I suspected anything,
it wasn't that. Yes it was odd,
that Grace being there just to sew,
get paid a king's ransom and not be sacked
for arson or attempted murder,
never mind being drunk on duty.
What could I do? I came off all right
in the end, though a mention on the last page
would have been nice. I often wonder
what would have happened
had the old place not burnt down,
whether I'd still be there.
It wasn't meant to be, as they say.

PETER J. DONNELLY

Dean Delaney descended from heaven with a cigar

Dean Delaney descended from heaven with a cigar,
hints of incense rolled in smoke haloed about him,
he sat in an armchair by our fire, larger than God,
leg crossed, ankle rested on a hefty knee, the chair sighed.

Eyes raised, I peeped over the dark sole of his boot,
along his trouser leg, onto his stomach's black expanse,
his chest heaved, rolling darkness, leading to a dash of
white
dog-collar peeping out its shrine, glowing, inserted beneath
a red face quietly inspecting me through huge spectacles,
probing for symptoms of venal sin masquerading as
innocence,
deeper, the everlasting trace of mortal sin, coiled, snoozing,
hidden from the light and my sight, sleeping in my warm
soul.

His hands clasped his knee, fingers bigger than clenched
fists spread
and contracted, a gold ring took me on a journey along his
knuckle,
above the black suit, the white dash, the red flesh, to a
dazzling yellow light,
fixed eyes burnt, pierced, concentrating, inquisitive, as if
scrutinising...
                              a specimen.

STEPHEN BECKETT-DOYLE

Glasgow

What other mess of houses, what other
divine assortment of stone, what other
2x2 and 4x4 collection
of windows, glass and door, would offer
Sebastian Munster's Cosmographia. For
emerging under a slice of orange
that bridges bright morning snow, Hillhead's
gauzy and gaudy yellow slip-ons
and firm slick black brogues beating a beat,
glance again at painted pride and glacial
facial recognition. Chauvet cogs
click quietly. Civically the circular
seeps. The national becomes the
universal at the Òran Mór.

You take a flick through it, crimping the new
A5 pages, in a newsagents on
Dumbarton Road. Sticky buns slowly stick,
sucking at slimy plastic. We could meet
at The Cabin Restaurant, take a risk,
order the salty lobster bisque. There you
can read the red headlines, the underground
sounds of *Call Me The Robinhood of
Kilsyth* or *Coffin Kept Closed*. I am
not *Scotland's First Hard Man* or a *Doorstep
Rat.* Half-baked *Alba*. Scorched toffee.
Handbagged *tablet*. Yet words like these
thread their urgent music with fresh ease.
A blunt trumpet cast in salt: *clear as day*.

Andrew Fletcher's pen paints a pretty
picture. The sodden ground, mulches of peat.
"It is only fit for the slaves who
sold it." Self-denying gripes of "colonised
and colonisers." A great foot swell that

delivers, moving across the great green
glaur, new *empórions* and fleshpots
for your *Tai-pans* and *Sahibs*.

"No straight thing was ever made," out
of the stone that refuses to melt
with the sun.

SAMUEL MCILHAGGA

The Amateur Mechanic's Pit

You built a pit in your home garage
to tend the undercarriage of cars.
How it was worth your while I dunno,

for the sake of the 'bangers' you owned:
the Ford Cortina 9 years after its release for instance,
or the white Anglia with stripes of Kerry's football colours.

The man from next door who was a busy-body/pain-in-
the-ass
joked that 'tis a grave you're building there, young-Mickie,
when he came to 'supervise' the pit building proceedings.

To us, your nephews, you were an old man at this time.
In reality you were only around fifty-three or so
but this neighbour still called you young-Mickie.

You even smoked down in your pit, so you did,
would've been dangerous I know, with the oil and petrol
spills.
You used Swarfega to wash your hands in a tin bucket first,

a second rinse under the outside tap and a 3rd wash in the
kitchen,
drying them with a towel your old mother, my Gran,
handed you.
Then you ate the dinner she cooked in the middle of the
day

before putting back on the overalls, stepping back into the
pit.
You only worked on it on wet days, gardens and meadows
on dry ones.
The pit was the only one of your activities I didn't tag along
on,

would hope the big black telephone in your mother's
parlour would ring,
calling you away for some reason, some errand I could join
in on.
Once, with a bright-red car all spruced up and road-
worthy,

I held the garage door open while you carefully drove her
out,
tentatively, like a new baby and you rolled over my big toe.
The pit I'm sure is still there, the roof of the shed over it

has probably fallen in by now, all grasses and reeds and
rats;
no more cars being made roadworthy, no oil on your hands
in the great garage in the sky Uncle Mickie-boy.

NOEL KING

Tribute to Lost Africans

I mean the ones who lie beneath the sea,
forests made of bone,
coral at the feet, red fallen fruit. Or are they jewels
nestled at the base of winding trunks?

Forests made of bone
cannot pull out mighty roots wending into silt,
nestled at the base of winding trunks,
rigid even with the ebb. The flow

cannot pull out mighty roots, wending into silt;
will not allow them to go free,
rigid even with the ebb, the flow.
Barnacles that hold them like a brace

will not allow them to go free,
to sing above the surface about the slaving ships,
barnacles that hold them like a brace.
Pulling back the tide – would it be possible

to sing above the surface about the slaving ships?
More boats, filled with a human weight, are
pulling back the tide. Would it be possible
to see the migrants as our kin? We can't afford to lose one

more. Boats filled with a human weight are
seen on news reports, pictures of the drowned, unnamed.
Impossible
to see the migrants as our kin. We can't afford to lose one
moment of our day to think about these strangers,

seen on news reports. Pictures of the drowned, unnamed, impossible
to care about for long. But does it haunt us every
moment of our day to think about these strangers,
I mean the ones who lie beneath the sea.

JENNY MITCHELL

Dullards

...but cursed are dullards whom no action stuns,
That they should be as stones.
Wretched are they and mean...
(Insensibility, Wilfred Owen.)

I read Owen's poem a long, long time ago; those dullards
stayed with me.
Then it dawned on me he was describing my people, my
family, me.

These are my family, my people, labourers,
peasants, factory and cannon fodder,
stretching back into the first blip of history.

Invisible, amounting to a shadow at most, the masses,
occasionally running riot for bread, gin, or revenge,
non-believers, but sacrificial lambs to some greater good.

It's all in a throw of the dice, just remember to duck,
this life comes down to good or bad luck,
some place, some time, a bullet with your name on it?
They are useful in a war; they can die en masse,
fixed bayonets plodding toward machine guns,
like a Saturday tumble back from the pub,

some lucky bastards return, they do not seem burdened
with slaughter, or medals and ribbons, tales of glory,
honour and courage, or horror, and all that jazz,
they just want to slip into a doorway for a sly fag.

Some even practice religion in an offhand way,
Sunday mass, a bit of kneeling, preaching and praying,

they will not let their children starve or run naked,
will rarely love them, while swearing they love them to
death.

They have no faith in God or humanity's idealistic
ingenuity,
they do not care for castles in the air, or a dead man's
dialectic,
I see them marching shoulder to shoulder, a winding mass
without end, from nowhere to nowhere with death, their
mate.

I see my brother looking for that doorway, a quick fag
in the dark, before dawn breaks when he must run, be off,
or beat time with the machine. My people prefer to rest
and pull the veil of insensibility about them,
maybe add a little booze to soothe their dullness

STEPHEN BECKETT-DOYLE

Hare

Hare knows a thousand stories.
She has collected them
over lifetimes.

Before she was a hare
she was a bright yellow poppy,
bobbing and bending
on an eyelash stem.
This was when she learned the stories
of the whispering grasses.

Before then, she was a nightjar,
flat in the dirt, sharp on the wing.
This was when she learned the stories
of the rising moon.

Once, she was a beam of copper
buried deep in the stone of the earth.
This was when she learned the stories
of the electric field.

She spent a long time as a plum tree,
a century of listening
to the slow alchemy of fruit.
This was when she learned the stories
of the brimming sun.

Before this, she was a white-tailed deer,
an endless wait, all-consuming
from wide eye to tendon to leaping spine.
This was when she learned the stories
of wolves.

Before this she was a warm desert wind,
driven by the sun, singed and spiralling.

This was when she learned the stories
of the liquid hills.

At one time she was the horizon.
This was when she learned the stories
of the longing of the heart.

She is trying
to figure out the world
through stories.

But she will only tell you one
if she hears a story in return.

AVEN WILDSMITH

Mitten

(on a Tudor child's knitted glove in the Museum of London)

Perhaps you lost this glove
in the same way we lose ours:
your small hand slipping
from your mother's grip
as you half-turn to see
ice glinting on the Thames' dark edge
or perhaps to chase the bright, speeding arc
of another child's hoop
as it bowls along the walkway towards the bridge.
Surely your mother, her hot, quick breath
clouding the chilly air,
reaches and seizes your collar before
you skip away through the crowd
before your thin shoulders turn
and you're borne along by the
joy of your curiosity
knowing she is following,
just there, just there

ROSEMARY APPLETON

"What were in the fairy ring at Howden Dyke?"

Some days, I find it skewering
the fairy ring with a glottal stop,
picking its grassy teeth
with a blackbird's beak.

On others, when weekday evenings
crumple the last of the light
into the chests of hollowed trees
and the lines in women's faces,

a flash of its pre-secular beauty
waits in parks and snickets and prams
filled by October rain. It scars
the clay with its chalky scent

and bathes in the upturned pool
of a dustbin lid. It builds its spire
from the dockyard's crane, crowned
with rust and stolen gold. I mistake

a catkin for melted wax in a minster
long burnt down to the county's bones.
It adjusts the hands on the clock
to suit the bonfire hour,

then guards the churchyard
in a place where gravestones
etch themselves, where the downy birch
shudders from the magnetic earth.

OLIVIA HODGSON

A November Morning

November wind
unforgiving with its brittle edge
blows rumpled wood pigeon into view
with his wide lilac breast and
steady curious gait,
Several others tumble in
making brave swoops and dives
with their thimble-like bodies
emptying through the air,
Here comes tree sparrow
with his cheeks pinched
in gothic blush
and nut hatch too
who makes a rival of everyone,
And so I wait and I watch for
although it is more or less
the same everyday
this dance is also always different
and never fails to smooth down
the upturned corners
of my morning mind.

ANNA VEITCH

Homecoming

You'll see me coming one evening in November
Past the hedges you would cut when I was young
And sweeping up, I'd follow behind.
You'll say it's good to see me - a start.
But we'll keep our distance
And follow government advice.

We'll talk about the autumn weather
And my job, and my mother,
I'll see her in the kitchen, unaware.
We'll have things to say, to remember
But they will go unsaid, stuck in a vice.
I won't touch your hand.

But you'll know how I feel,
Despite the inarticulate speech of the heart
As we see the sun starting to give up.
So, there we'll stand at close of day
Two metres apart, still behind, shy,
Not knowing what else to say

(And not needing to say it twice)

You'll say, "go to your mother", through autumn leaves, two
metres apart, with that cascading feeling in my throat, my
heart.

SHANE OLIVER

Here we are again

It's December 15th and here I am again standing at your grave
The day you died.
It's a golden opportunity to speak while you listen but I don't have much to say.

This morning, I made porridge like you taught me when you used the Chinese cup
I don't have it anymore, so it never quite works out as well
And the measurements other people tell me are just rubbish.
You were an engineer after all.
Not that porridge really needs a slide rule
And anyway you were the only living person that knew how to use it.

But the Golden syrup from the tin
Was so solid, it was like I'd left it in from 1975.
A piece of amber drops slowly from a height into the boiling oats...
'Don't do that!' you would have said 'You'll make a mess'
I was always making a mess.

I look about under the blue sky in the Richmond cemetery.
There is no one here but me and the dead
And an eerie sense of Springtime out of season

And I remember the moment the grave digger appeared with his barrow
On the day of your burial like a scene from Hamlet
The others had gone, and I stood there with the snowdrops round your grave

And he asked me 'Do you want to put anything in?'
'I've nothing with me' I replied.
But he waited.

So, I put my hand in my pocket and there it was
The smiling face of John Paul II on a prayer card.

'From your part of the world, dad'
And your arch enemy for my affections, so you thought.
'Well dad, I'm sorry, but this is my final opportunity to have
the last word
So, he's coming in.'

And with a sense of having given you the best I had
I left you there in better hands than mine.

But here we are again, and I need to ask you so many
things about why the world's gone mad
And you'd reach then for The Times Atlas of World History
Which we eventually bought you for Christmas though we
knew we'd never hear the end of it.
What parallel would you find... the Magyars, or the Mayans,
the 50 million dead or Mao Tse Tung?
The movement of peoples over millions of years, all looking
for resources and a masterplan
Looking for an answer to the place where I now stand.
Beside you once again and waiting,
Waiting for your reply.

SARAH DE NORDWALL

The End of the Century at Parliament Hill

Lit in the mid-winter sun the park slopes down,
A lush, mown green, to where a football game
Is going on. Kindled in gold, the thorns have grown
As tall as trees; the brickwork is aflame,
The windows flash. The game ends in the last
Blaze of the sun. A local train grunts past.

In the enclosure, the mothers have begun
To make for home. The bikes and cars and toys
Are gathered up... *Take care, love... See you again
In the next century...* A laugh, lost in the noise
Of aircraft. Soon they'll be home, the kids asleep,
Their luck twice blessed with promises to keep.

They hurry on. Then suddenly the earth
Goes black, a crack of thunder cleaves the sky.
And through the ensuing silence billows forth
A terrible howl. And dies, leaving the cry
Of a child which spreads infinitely as if
The seas spoke, each wave bursting with fresh grief.

Ragged and grey the light returns. Someone
Slams a gate. Another train goes by.
A child waves at it. The lamps come on.
Such lives as these were those, ordinary,
Busy, decent, kind... One stops to stare
At shrivelled knots of fruit the brambles bear.

Do you remember, darling, that's where we picked
Blackberries in September and you pricked
Your finger and you cried and blood came?
Next year, I promise, it will be the same.

CHARLES CHADWICK

Anything Can be Anything
(for Rebecca)

Shimmering with frozen things,
she is about to go in
for a last-minute interview thing.
Her sweaty hand debates the doorknob
to open the
company. She, in her heart of hearts, starts to think of
poetry.
With poetry, she is no longer nervous, or thinks she won't
get the job. With poetry, anything can be anything
the doorknob can be a vulnerable silver hedgehog,
its spikes are so dense, making a perfect circle. Anything
can be anything
she pushes out the taste of doubt lurking beneath weeping
cells in distant lungs.
Think of poetry, think of poetry.

Her mouth won't tremble, but instead lips
move as if god is etching his signature on the required slot
of her mouth
He gestures with a flick of his wrist to sit down,
as if pointing to the indifference
of where she sits.
Her forehead isn't sweating, she is just letting the darkness
rain out
so she can negotiate rainbows over -*would you like water
or coffee or tea?*
while she wonders diplomatically if the beverage is part of
the test, *water thanks*
Stroking silver hedgehogs in her hands.

LANA MASTERSON

Gower Street School

I remember rooms
Charlotte Mew, pupil in the 1870s who later died by suicide.

How wide the world seems, here.
She sits and listens as all the while the
pale sun moves across the window panes,
bathing the crowns of the plane trees
and Miss Harrison marches them
through Virgil's weighted lines,
the syllables chiming like bells, all
searching, striving, grief, regret –

and she learns how a voice can inhabit a room,
and that to die can be an action,
not just a fading or a passing on,
that there might be a moment, just before,
when one's own voice sounds, suddenly clear,
finds its pitch the way a note,
held on a string, tautens into tune,
to then be heard, hymned, remembered.

ROSEMARY APPLETON

À deux
(for Nicholas Phillipson)

I meant to say I won't be there
with you, mutual senses reaching
as, with head bent back,
we traverse a lofty peacock-blue and ivory painted ceiling.

You won't have thought before about this - but I did,
side-by-side, à deux on a wooden pew
to celebrate a life or all life,
referred to as much the same on these occasions.

I meant to say I won't be there and neither will you be
actually,
here at the Chapel of Remembrance
now wrapped up for the day
to obey that inscription inscribed on the window;
'Night has come and there will be no more work'.

No more work. No more dark outfits,
no more sadness, infernal preoccupations.
No more exhumation,
prising open our hard-fought entrancements of love.

That sip of water from a carafe lay-readers and relatives
reach for,
will by now have been spirited off.
Tunes by Schubert, Ed Sheeran will have muted.
Best of all, there will be no fresh casket.

Although I won't be there and neither will you,
I meant to say how much
I was already thinking about this occasion and to all of you
here
who will be dealing with the future.
I know you were expecting me to participate.

So the best I can assure you of, those of you
caught up in that transposition,
when with sense-consciousness, we look around seeing
elements of the living sensed back,
ready to transmit like a glass of water or much-admired
song,

when voiceless, joined feelings resonate under a peacock-
blue and ivory painted ceiling,
would be how I unaccountably understand this
about every single one of you here at some level
and however ridiculously.

DAMON MOORE

The shape and size of my sister's coffin

Against the wall, near the door
a wooden radiogram appeared unexpectantly.

Under its lid, a swivelled radio dial searched
the outside world for words, songs, to fill   the void.

We waited
for the LP record
to slump onto the deck.

We entered its silence
between the gentle descent of the needle,
and that first kiss of contact

and Johnny Cash's 'Ring of Fire'
galloped out, the length of the living room.

Whenever her name was mentioned
the arm was abruptly lifted
              mid song.

MEL MCEVOY

ACKNOWLEDGEMENTS

This anthology would not be possible without the support of countless writers all over the UK and Ireland, some of whom are students, working in healthcare, seeking employment, aspiring writers or already published poets – all of them entrusted us with their work and I am indebted to our judges who had the impossible task of settling on poems for inclusion in this anthology or for selecting the prize winners. I am very lucky to have had their guidance throughout this project. The talent across the UK and Ireland is phenomenal and this book could only provide a snapshot of the hundreds of entries we received – there are numerous more who demonstrated great skill in writing poetry, and we hope we have the opportunity in future to promote their work and see their careers flourish. Poetry is not dead. I would like to thank every media publication that helped spread the word – we once feared before embarking on this journey that we would not receive sufficient entries, but those fears were soon allayed by the generosity of editors, journalists, and writers such as Brendan Walsh, Ruth Gledhill, Dan Carrier, Fiona Audley, Elizabeth Mohen and the team at Poetry Ireland, Paddy Casey, Bridget Galton, Dennis Relojo-Howell, Bernard Purcell, and Lorraine Mariner and the team at the National Poetry Library in London. For their time and support, I am extremely grateful. Thank you to my family, friends, neighbours and the online community who helped in all sorts of ways to encourage me to follow this project to the end. Thank you to everyone who bought this book. I hope it does some good – proceeds will go to Pancreatic Cancer UK, in solidarity with every healthcare worker and in thanks to you for buying this book. – *M.C., February 2021.*

NOTES ON THE CONTRIBUTORS

Amy Gillies is a contemporary artist, who lives and works in London. Employing painting and poetry as a vehicle for social and political dialogue, her practice is concerned with the memory of the past and the politics of the present. In 2019, Amy completed an MFA in Fine Art at Kingston School of Art. Since graduating, Amy has performed at Bermondsey Project Space and has taken part in the Artist in Residence programme at One Paved Court.

Anna Beddow lives in Manchester her adopted home although the Black Country is where her heart belongs. She began writing poetry seriously a few years ago whilst maintaining a day job in education.

Anna Margarita Veitch is an anthropologist, visual artist and poet based in the North East of England. Her work is most greatly inspired by the woodlands, fields, plants, and creatures that are at the heart of her life and seeks to explore the experiences of emotional solace, freedom, and healing that a mindful and curious reconnection with wilder elements of being can bring. She is currently working on her first collection of poetry which she intends to self-publish.

Aoife O'Connor is a writer and teacher based in Dublin. In 2020, her work was published in two anthologies and this year her poetry was chosen to form part of an art instillation by Nickie Hayden titled 'Haiku Sanctuary'. Her poem 'Transfer' explores the change in dynamic when a parent becomes sick and the passing of responsibility to create a new leader in the family. It was written during a period when her partner was supporting a friend through this transition.

Aven Wildsmith is a writer and artist from Devon. Their writing explores the way we understand our fears and desires through folklore and myth. They can often be found reading spooky stories, singing badly, and taking pictures of trees. Find them on Instagram @avenwildsmith

Becky Ciesielski gathers, coaxes and stitches fragments of memory and experience into a new whole, whether in her writing, visual art or weaving. And, occasionally, some everyday magic seeps through the seams...Having grown up in London, Becky is now settled in a tiny village in the North York Moors. Amidst the wildness of the moors, she lives in an old cottage with her wife, dog, several chickens, and a growing collection of handwoven coasters.

Beth Brooke is a retired teacher, born in the Middle East but now living near Dorset's amazing Jurassic Coast. She loves poetry, her sons, and the sea. She can be found on Twitter @BethBrooke8.

Beth Finney is a freelance writer, editor and poet based in London, UK. Intrigued by the minute details of everyday life, she seeks out earnest, snapshot moments to expand and write about in depth. She is currently Deputy Editor at Oceanographic Magazine and is a proud alumnus of the Write Like a Grrrl creative courses.

Briony Collins is a poet, novelist, and playwright. She won the 2016 Exeter Novel Prize and has several prominent publications. Her debut poetry pamphlet, Blame It On Me, is forthcoming with Broken Sleep Books in August 2021. She is co-founder and co-editor of Cape Magazine. Briony is currently a Pushcart Prize nominee and is represented by DHH Literary Agency.

Carol Sheppard lives in the beautiful Forest of Dean, UK and loves to walk amongst the trees. Animals and the beauty of nature inspires much of her poetry.

Charles Chadwick spent nine years in the Overseas Civil Service in Zambia, followed by twenty-five years with the British Council in Kenya, Nigeria, Brazil, Canada, and Poland. He is the author of novels It's All Right Now (Faber) and A Chance Acquaintance, also published in the USA, France and Germany, and has had three other novels published in Germany. He was first a resident of Hampstead, London some 53 years ago.

Christina Lewis lives in Glasgow and began writing regularly during the UK's first lockdown. She loves writing poems whilst going for walks around her local park. She also loves reading, listening to podcasts (often during walks), eating ice cream, and hillwalking (she walks a lot). She writes under her mother's surname to represent the important influence of women on both her work and her identity. This is her first published piece, but she has aspirations for many more.

Ciorsdan Glass has a Master's degree in Creative Writing from Oxford University and an undergraduate in English Literature and Philosophy from Trinity College Dublin. She works in NHS Communications and is head of digital at Poems in the Waiting Room. Her poem is dedicated to all those who lost their lives or loved ones in the Grenfell fire and to all those striving to make sure that such a disaster does not happen again.

Coriander Stuttard's poetry has previously been published in the South Bank Poetry Magazine. As well as writing creatively, she also spends her professional time writing about classical music and has a keen interest in mental health and the arts. Coriander has grown up walking on Hampstead Heath and now enjoys spending time observing and photographing its nature and life with her two daughters and their dog.

Damon Moore co-manages an artist's studio project in Frome, Somerset. He has a particular interest in narrative and extended poetry whilst his short-form poems have appeared in journals and magazines including Wildness, Porridge, Fly on the Wall and FENCE. His poems commonly have a strong connection to setting, À Deux being composed at Warriston Chapel in north Edinburgh.

Danuta Orlowska works in the NHS as a clinical psychologist alongside inspirational patients and colleagues. Outside work she dabbles in abstract art. She is keen to get back to Scottish and French country dancing and is looking forward to travelling around Scotland.

Dave Bevan breaks skateboards and bikes for fun and fixes bikes for rent. He lives on a boat where the Trent skirts Nottingham.

Dominic Fisher has been published in a wide variety of poetry magazines and been successful in several competitions. His collection The Ladies and Gentlemen of the Dead was published by The Blue Nib in 2019. He is a co-editor of Raceme and a member of the site-specific poetry performance group called the IsamBards. dominicfisherpoetry.com

Greg Smith is a retired Technical Author and lives in Harpenden. He completed the MA in Writing Poetry at the Poetry School in 2018. He is an active member of the Ver Poets committee and is the treasurer and membership secretary. Recently, he won third prize in the Poetry Space competition and has had poems published in the Alchemy Spoon and the Brian Dempsey Memorial Competition anthology.

Hartley Lloyd Pack is a poet, musician and teacher. In 2016 he released Sixteen Sunsets, an album which blended poetry, rap, and choral singing, featuring contributions from Sam Lee, TRILLS, and Jehane Markham. In 2018 Hartley launched Mixtape Assembly, a podcast in which artists talk about the songs that have most meaningful in their lives, with guests including Benjamin Zephaniah and Mighty Moe. Hartley is currently developing Raw Gods, a narrative poem which has been inspired by his work supporting young people living in Care in Hackney. His can be found on

Instagram @hartleylloydpack (and mixtapeassembly.com and sixteensunsets.bandcamp.com)

Helen Openshaw is a Drama and English teacher, living in Cumbria. She enjoys writing poetry and plays and inspiring her students in their creative writing. Helen had a short monologue commissioned by Knock and Nash productions last year. This is her first published poem, and hopefully the start of many!

J.D. Murray is a support worker from Kilburn. He's interested in working with legendary material, and is currently engaged in rendering the medieval Robin Hood ballads into modern English.

Jenny Mitchell is winner of the Folklore Prize, Aryamati Prize, the Segora Prize, a Bread and Roses Poetry Award, the Fosseway Prize; and joint winner of the Geoff Stevens Memorial Prize 2019. Her poems have been published widely, and a debut collection, Her Lost Language (Indigo Dreams Publishing) is one of 44 Poetry Books for 2019 (Poetry Wales); and a Jhalak Prize #bookwelove. A forthcoming collection, Map of a Plantation (IDP), will be published in April 2021. Twitter: @jennymitchellgo

Jim Mulligan, eighty-five, has form as a writer. He served time as head of English at Pimlico school, got respectability with an MA in writing at Middlesex University, won a kind of fame by being the only winner of the Ham & High short story competition. They only ran it for one year. He has had three plays put on in London fringe theatres and acted with Spare Tyre - once at the Edinburgh Festival and with Old Vic New Voices.

Kerry Darbishire lives in Cumbria. Her collections: A Lift of Wings 2014 & Distance Sweet on my Tongue 2018 (Finalist: Cumbria Culture Awards 2019) Indigo Dreams. Her biography Kay's Ark 2016 Handstand Press. Her poems appear widely in anthologies and magazines and have won prizes including shortlisted Bridport 2017. Her third collection Jardinière won Hedgehog Press Collection Prize, to be published 2022. The Cumbria Opera Group will be performing her poetry in September 2021. Twitter: @kerrydarbishire

Lana Belle Masterson is a poet and historical fiction bookworm living in Cardiff. During her time in London, she was a Barbican Young Poet, featuring in two Barbican Young Poet anthologies. She has performed her poetry in Milton Court Concert Hall, The Barbican Centre, The Library in Trafalgar Square, Ironbridge Festival and The Ritzy Cinema in Brixton. More of her work can be found at lanawritesalot.blogspot.com. Her recent poetry is very much inspired by reading Lucinda Riley, Anthony Doerr, Brene Brown and Maya Angelou.

Libby Chandler is 23 years old and writes for enjoyment in her spare time. This is her first published piece. Beginning full-time work after college with no definitive direction, she clung to the creative outlets she has cherished since childhood. Libby continues to express herself and connect creatively, channelling her imagination through written words.

Lynne Wycherley lives near a headland in Devon and has long been inspired by light and landscape. Although her health has flickered in recent years, her lyrical poetry has continued to appear in loved poetry journals. Her main collection Listening to Light was published by Shoestring Press in 2014, edited by John Lucas, in 2014; her Brooksong and Shadows is due from Shoestring later this year. She is married to a musician and is active in various health charities.

Max Hallam lives in Uxbridge, the last strip of suburb clinging onto the sprawl of London proper. After growing up on a steady diet of Jenny Nimmo and Robin Hobb, he now writes stories with speculative twists which ground the eerie in the urban, the mythical in the mundane. His short story Hylätä won the 2019 Hillingdon Literary Festival.

Mel McEvoy was born in Liverpool in 1959 to Irish immigrants. He spent five years in Catholic religious life. Still a nurse after 38 years in the NHS, mainly in End-of-Life Care. First collection of poems 'An Emptied Space' published by Mudfog (2012). Master of Arts in Creative Writing Open University (2019). Three poems in 'These are the hands' NHS Anthology March (2020). Currently involved in collaborative research with the OU promoting creative writing in acute hospital settings.

Natalie Crick has poems published in Stand, The Moth, Banshee, Agenda and elsewhere. She is studying for an MPhil in Creative Writing at Newcastle University and is poetry editor for Fragmented Voices small press. Natalie's poetry was commended in the Verve Poetry Festival Competition 2020 and awarded second prize in the Newcastle Poetry Competition 2020. One of her poems received a special mention by judge Ilya Kaminsky in the Poetry London Prize 2020. Follow her on twitter @PoetryNatalie.

Nicole Charleston is a third year Creative and Professional Writing student at the University of Winchester. Whilst working on a collection of poetry for her dissertation, she has had a handful of poems published in 1998 Magazine. 'Summer, 2020' is a poem that is part of one of Nicole's module assignments, a collection called City. Aside from writing, she works part time in retail and hopes to study a masters in a humanities subject when she graduates.

Olivia Hodgson completed her MA in Creative Writing at Birmingham City University where she won the Mercian Prize for Poetry. She has poems published in Strix, Dreich, Littoral Press Magazine, The Lyrical Aye, The Honest Ulsterman, and Crow and Cross Keys.

Peter J Donnelly lives in York and has degrees in English and Creative Writing from the University of Wales Lampeter. He has been published in several magazines including Southlight, South Bank, Dreich, Writer's Egg, Poetry Village and the Beach Hut. His work has also appeared in various poetry anthologies including the Dare to Create 'Lockdown Rhythm'. He was recently awarded joint runner up in the Buzzwords open poetry competition for his poem 'The Second of August'.

Petra Markham is an actor. Her films include Get Carter (1971) and The Hireling and her theatre includes Equus and Lettice and Lovage in 2017 directed by Trevor Nunn. She has written a radio play which she is submitting and has been writing a play about the poet Charlotte Mew. She is also beginning to write a story for children with her own illustrations. Dreaming is her first poem to be published.

Philip Burton has been a Lancashire head teacher and a poetry practitioner for children. In 2019 he concurrently held four poetry competition First prizes, including Sandwich (Kent) Poet of the Year. Philip was recently awarded a Commendation by Heidi Williamson in the 2020 Poetry Society Stanza competition. His poetry publications include The Raven's Diary (joe publish 1998), Couples (Clitheroe Books Press 2008), His Usual Theft, (Indigo Dreams Press 2017) and Gaia Warnings (Palewell Press 2021).

Randall Stephens is a writer with a banking background who has since found an interest in books, spending time in libraries, and working by the seaside.

Rebecca Baird is a Scottish poet and journalist based in Dundee. Her writing focuses mainly on music, the mythologizing of feminine experience and the romance of the mundane. You can usually find her among trees, fairy lights or gravestones, writing things in her head, or her notes app.

Richard Pilkington, born in Bolton, is an ex-advertising man who became a musician who became a poet. His advertising career won awards for tv and radio commercials including Kronenbourg, John Smiths and his accidental naming of the 8 Out of 10 Cats comedy panel show. His musical life in The Blackheart Orchestra (theblackheartorchestra.com) continues to win awards for both their albums and live shows. The river flowed into his lockdown love affair with poetry, and now, nine months after writing his first poem in a Glasgow hospital, his poetry has found its voice in exploring the real emotions dwelling within seemingly simple everyday personal experiences. His words are heartfelt, self-reflective, passionate, and unadulterated by adherence to poetic style or structure.

Robert Ilson is an Honorary Research Fellow of University College London, sometime Associate Director of its Survey of English Usage, and a writer, editor, language-teacher, and lexicographer doomed at last to wake a poet (as Samuel

Johnson was "a poet doomed at last to wake a lexicographer").

Rosemary Appleton lives in Suffolk and writes in snatched moments, fuelled by coffee. She has twice been a winner of the Oxford Radcliffe Library Science & Poetry Prize and her work has appeared in Mslexia, The Fenland Reed, Black Bough Poems, The Wellington Street Journal and elsewhere. Her poems are anthologised by Dunlin Press, PaperSwans, and Fairacre Press.

S. M. L. Yau is a British poet and writer of Chinese descent based in the West Midlands. She spent her early life in Hong Kong before returning to the UK. She is an educator and has written reclusively for eight years, predominantly on her identity, life and upbringing. She can be found on Instagram (@smlyau_poetry) and is working on her debut poetry collection, 'Descended from salt water.'.

Sam Smith is passionate about the power of poetry and, in the words of Denise Riley, wrote to 'earth her heart' after losing both her parents in the Covid Pandemic. A person-centred Therapist with a special interest in Bibliotherapy, she lives and works in Hampshire. Sam has had work published by Ice Floe Press, Post Script, Poetry and Covid, and Analogies and Allegories Literary Magazine. She is on Twitter as @Fictionprescri1.

Samuel McIlhagga is a recent graduate of the University of Cambridge. He was shortlisted for the Jane Martin Poetry

Prize in 2016 and edited the poetry section of The Mays in 2020. He works as a financial and political journalist.

Sarah DeNordwall was inspired by tales of the 8th century bards of Ireland to become a Bard with a Bard School. Being 1,200 years too late to join one, she had to set one up herself. During Covid-time she has run a writing class for the homeless around Mayfair and also curated five Bardic Mic nights online called "When Joy Begins". She won the Wild Words poetry competition in 2019 and her book "A Beginner's Guide to Opening the World with Words" is available on Audible. www.sarahdenordwall.com

Sarah Jane O'Hare is a poet, expressive arts facilitator and embodiment coach. She recently co-founded Creation Poetry, an modern and inclusive online poetry community where she hosts monthly open mics, workshops, and more. She's currently working on her debut poetry book, A Witch without Honey. ohsarahjane.co.uk

Steve Denehan lives in Kildare, Ireland with his wife Eimear and daughter Robin. He is the author of two chapbooks and two poetry collections. Twice winner of Irish Times' New Irish Writing, his numerous publication credits include Poetry Ireland Review, Acumen, Prairie Fire, Westerly and Into the Void. He has been nominated for Best of the Net, Best New Poet and The Pushcart Prize.

Stephen Beckett-Doyle, born in 1950, in industrial Bolton, went to Catholic Schools, leaving school at 16. The industrial world (deceased), the moorland around Bolton and Catholicism are influential on his outlook. His working life was a mixture of labouring and clerical jobs, living mostly in London. He is an avid reader and occasional writer. He lives in Suffolk. In brief: half-man half-dreamer, a Catholic who does not believe in God.

Vanessa Lampert has an MA in Writing Poetry from Newcastle University and Poetry School London. In 2020 she came first in the Café Writers and Ver Poetry Prizes, and second in the Fish and Oxford Brookes Prizes She has been published widely in magazines, most recently in Magma, Quince, The Moth, Spoonfeed and The Oxford Times. Vanessa's first pamphlet 'On Long Loan' was published by Live Canon in October 2020. She co-edits and writes for the online and print magazine The Alchemy Spoon. Vanessa lives in Oxfordshire and works as an acupuncturist.

Zara Al-Noah is a former research scientist, now training as a physician associate in the NHS. She has only very recently started writing poetry, the Folklore Prize being her first submission. She has found it a cathartic outlet to stem the emotions of both work and motherhood. Her work is pending publication in various anthologies and she is looking forward to expanding her love of writing. (Instagram: @littlepocketpoems).

THIS BOOK IS DEDICATED TO THE MEMORY OF
ALBERT ADAMS (1929-2006)

Ape
(for Albert, for Ted)

You showed me a picture of an ape, and I listened to you
explain it was drawn from memory after his childhood toy.
When I looked at the ape it seemed sad, sick, and blue,
like it knew the world would hurt its owner.

Days later you were in an ambulance on Albert Street,
telling the crew to take off your watches (you wore two)
and give them to me to keep safe, now at my bedside, tick,
tick, and tick – safe from harm – a charm, a heartbeat.

I can almost see you now in your bed in the Royal Free,
nurses at your blue and metal bed, you look at the ceiling,
thinking of Camden, of places, of people,
of home, of Albert, of faces, drawn from memory.

MARTIN CONNOLLY

Printed in Great Britain
by Amazon